LEONARD BERNSTEIN

CHICHESTER PSALMS

(In Three Movements)

For Mixed Choir (or Male Choir), Boy Solo and Orchestra

(to be sung in Hebrew)

Vocal Score

LEONARD
BERNSTEIN
Music Publishing
Company LLC

BOOSEY & HAWKES

FOREWORD

Every summer the Cathedral of Chichester, in Sussex, England, joins choral forces with its neighbors, Winchester and Salisbury, to produce a music festival. (Chichester has a great musical tradition, going back to its famed organist-composer of the early 17th century, Thomas Weelkes.) For its 1965 Festival, Leonard Bernstein was commissioned to write these *Psalms*, which were completed on May 7, 1965. The world premiere took place on July 15, 1965, in Philharmonic Hall, New York, with the composer conducting the New York Philharmonic, with the Camerata Singers, Abraham Kaplan, conductor, and with John Bogart, alto. The first performance of the original version, as conceived by Mr. Bernstein for all-male choir, was heard on July 31, 1965, at Chichester.

J. G.

COMPOSER'S NOTE

The soprano and alto parts are written with boys' voices in mind. It is possible, though not preferable, to substitute women's voices. There are a few passages for solo voices, which may be sung by individuals of the choir. However, the long male-alto solo in the second movement must not be sung by a woman, but either by a boy or a counter-tenor.

L. B.

LEONARD BERNSTEIN® is a registered trademark of
The Leonard Bernstein Music Publishing Company LLC, Publisher

Commissioned by the Very Rev. Walter Hussey, Dean of Chichester Cathedral, Sussex,
for its 1965 Festival, and dedicated, with gratitude, to Cyril Solomon

CONTENTS

TEXT

I

Ps. 108, vs. 2:

Urah, hanevel, v'chinor!	Awake, psaltery and harp:
A-irah shahar!	I will rouse the dawn!

Ps. 100, entire:

Hariu l'Adonai kol haarets.	Make a joyful noise unto the Lord all ye lands.
Iv'du et Adonai b'simha.	Serve the Lord with gladness.
Bo-u l'fanav bir'nanah.	Come before His presence with singing.
D'u ki Adonai Hu Elohim.	Know ye that the Lord, He is God.
Hu asanu, v'lo anahnu.	It is He that hath made us, and not we ourselves.
Amo v'tson mar'ito.	We are His people and the sheep of His pasture.
Bo-u sh'arav b'todah,	Enter into His gates with thanksgiving,
Hatseirotav bit'hilah,	And into His courts with praise.
Hodu lo, bar'chu sh'mo.	Be thankful unto Him, and bless His name.
Ki tov Adonai, l'olam has'do,	For the Lord is good, His mercy is everlasting,
V'ad dor vador emunato.	And His truth endureth to all generations.

II

Ps. 23, entire:

Adonai ro-i, lo ehsar.	The Lord is my shepherd, I shall not want.
Bin'ot deshe yarbitseini,	He maketh me to lie down in green pastures,
Al mei m'nuhot y'nahaleini,	He leadeth me beside the still waters,
Naf'shi y'shovev,	He restoreth my soul,
Yan'heini b'ma'aglei tsedek,	He leadeth me in the paths of righteousness,
L'ma'an sh'mo.	For His name's sake.
Gam ki eilech	Yea, though I walk
B'gei tsalmavet,	Through the valley of the shadow of death,
Lo ira ra,	I will fear no evil,
Ki Atah imadi.	For Thou art with me.
Shiv't'cha umishan'techa	Thy rod and Thy staff
Hemah y'nahamuni.	They comfort me.
Ta'aroch l'fanai shulchan	Thou preparest a table before me
Neged tsor'rai	In the presence of mine enemies,
Dishanta vashemen roshi	Thou anointest my head with oil,
Cosi r'vayah.	My cup runneth over.
Ach tov vahesed	Surely goodness and mercy
Yird'funi kol y'mei hayai,	Shall follow me all the days of my life,
V'shav'ti b'veit Adonai	And I will dwell in the house of the Lord
L'orech yamim.	Forever.

Ps. 2, vs. 1-4:

Lamah rag'shu goyim	Why do the nations rage,
Ul'umim yeh'gu rik?	And the people imagine a vain thing?
Yit'yats'vu malchei erets,	The kings of the earth set themselves,
V'roznim nos'du yahad	And the rulers take counsel together
Al Adonai v'al m'shiho.	Against the Lord and against His anointed.
N'natkah et mos'roteimo,	Saying, let us break their bands asunder,
V'nashlichah mimenu avoteimo.	And cast away their cords from us.
Yoshev bashamayim	He that sitteth in the heavens
Yis'hak, Adonai	Shall laugh, and the Lord
Yil'ag lamo!	Shall have them in derision!

Ps. 131, entire:	*Adonai, Adonai,*	Lord, Lord,
	Lo gavah libi,	My heart is not haughty,
	V'lo ramu einai,	Nor mine eyes lofty,
	V'lo hilachti	Neither do I exercise myself
	Big'dolot uv'niflaot	In great matters or in things
	Mimeni.	Too wonderful for me.
	Im lo shiviti	Surely I have calmed
	V'domam'ti,	And quieted myself,
	Naf'shi k'gamul alei imo,	As a child that is weaned of his mother,
	Kagamul alai naf'shi.	My soul is even as a weaned child.
	Yahel Yis'rael el Adonai	Let Israel hope in the Lord
	Me'atah v'ad olam.	From henceforth and forever.
Ps. 133, vs. 1:	*Hineh mah tov,*	Behold how good,
	Umah naim,	And how pleasant it is,
	Shevet ahim	For brethren to dwell
	Gam yahad.	Together in unity.

—◆◆—

PRONUNCIATION GUIDE
(for the Hebrew transliteration)

1. All vowels (and diphthongs) as in Italian.

2. All consonants as in English, except:

    H   — slightly guttural H, though not
            as guttural as

    CH, which is pronounced as in German (Buch).

    R   — rolled, if possible, as in Italian.

    '   — appearing after a consonant, as in Y'
            or L', is to be regarded as a vowel,
            and given syllabic value whenever
            indicated by a note or grace-note. It
            is a "neutral" vowel, rather like the
            mute E in French. Where syllabic value
            is not indicated, ' is to be ignored.

INSTRUMENTATION

3 Trumpets in B♭
3 Trombones
Timpani
Percussion (5)*
2 Harps
Strings

*glockenspiel, xylophone, chimes, triangle,
wood block, temple blocks, tambourine,
snare drum, 3 bongos, bass drum, cymbals,
suspended cymbal, whip, rasp

Duration: 18½ minutes

Performance materials are available from the Boosey & Hawkes Rental Library

A full score (FSB-467) and pocket score (HPS-1201) are available for sale

A reduction of the orchestration for organ, harp and percussion
is available for sale (ENB-264)

The First Movement of *Chichester Psalms* is published separately for
SATB chorus with keyboard accompaniment (OCTB-6347)

RECORDINGS

Original Version:
John Bogart (boy alto), Camerata Singers (Abraham Kaplan, director),
New York Philharmonic, Leonard Bernstein
Columbia ML 6192/MS 6792 (E,G,I) CBS 72374

Boy Alto from Wiener Sängerknaben, Wiener Jeunesse Chor (Günther
Teuring, director), Israel Philharmonic, Leonard Bernstein
DG 2530968, DG 2709077 (with "Jeremiah" Symphony)
DG CD 415965-2 (with "Songfest")

Aled Jones (boy alto), London Symphony Chorus, Royal Philharmonic
Orchestra, Richard Hickox
RPO-MCA Classics MCAD-6199

Arranged for Organ, Harp and Percussion:
James Bowman (counter-tenor), King's College Choir of Cambridge, Phillip Ledger;
James Lancelot, organ; Osian Ellis, harp; David Corkhill, percussion
Angel S 37119, (E) HMV ASD 3035

Chichester Psalms

I
Psalm 108, vs. 2
Psalm 100, entire

LEONARD BERNSTEIN

Corrected Edition February 1991
Printed in U.S.A.

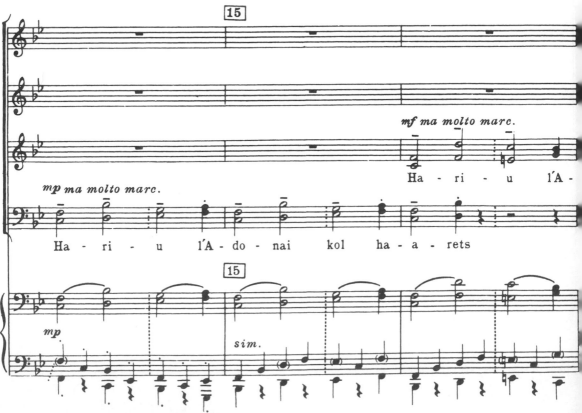

4

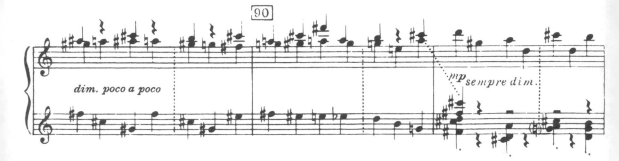

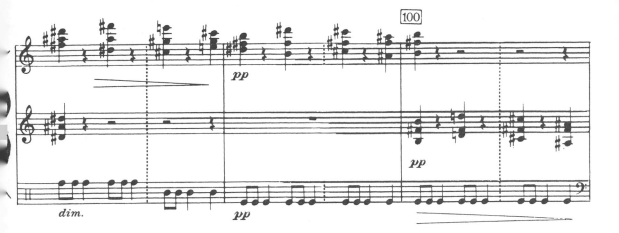

II
Psalm 23. entire
Psalm 2. vs. 1-4

*Fewer voices than the upper part.

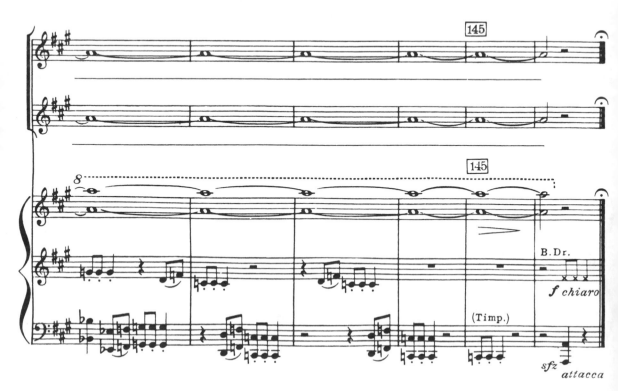

III

Psalm 131, entire
Psalm 133, vs. 1

Prelude

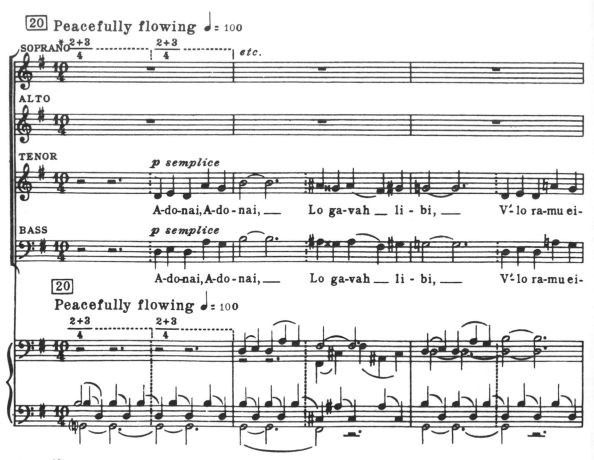

* This $\frac{10}{4}$ should be conducted in the *shape* of a divided 4 beat, adding an extra inner beat on 2 and 4 (1 + 2 ++, 3 + 4 ++).

U - mah ___ na - im, She - vet a - him

U - mah ___ na - im, She - vet a - him

U - mah na - im, She - vet a - him

U - mah ___ na - im, She - vet a - him

pppp Gam ya-had, gam ya-had. ___ A - men. ___

pppp Gam ya-had, gam ya-had. ___ A - men. ___

pppp Gam ya-had, gam ya-had. ___ A - men. ___

pppp Gam ya-had, gam ya-had. ___ A - men. ___

poco lunga poss.

pp dolce

pp

lunga poss.

ppp lunga poss.

Fairfield, Conn.
April-May 1965